WELCOME TO A WONDERFUL WORLD OF STICKERS!

The **JUNGLE** is one of nature's most amazing habitats, full of fascinating creatures and plants. Use the stickers in this book to create your own **SAFARI** – from brilliant beasts that **SQUAWK**, **HISS**, **GROWL** and **ROAR**, to carnivorous **PLANTS** and beautiful **BLOOMS**.

Simply match each numbered sticker at the back of the book to the same number in the sticker grid!

sticker grid

You can even customise the scenes with some of the extra stickers at the back.

Learn fun facts about each of the creatures and plants you create!

Use the checklist at the back of the book to tick off the things you find next time you venture into the wild!

sticker sheet

Eventually, you'll have a whole jungle to explore!

Note: The sticker sheets can be pulled out so that you don't have to keep flicking to the end. Stickers are slightly larger than the areas they cover so no awkward white bits show through.

BEETLES

The **HORNED DUNG BEETLE** is the strongest insect in the world. It can pull an object weighing a whopping 1,141 times its body weight. That's the equivalent of a full-grown human dragging 65 cars!

Beetles have strong **ARMOUR** to protect their **WINGS**.

Beetles can chew through tough foliage using their powerful **PINCER-LIKE JAWS**.

There are more than **4,200** beetle species in the UK.

COLOUR WITH STICKERS

NATURE

JUNGLE

FSC
www.fsc.org
MIX
Paper from
responsible sources
FSC® C135401

The Forest Stewardship Council® (FSC®) is an international, non-governmental organisation dedicated to promoting responsible management of the world's forests. FSC operates a system of forest certification and product labelling that allows consumers to identify wood and wood-based products from well-managed forests and other controlled sources.

For more information about the FSC, please visit their website at www.fsc.org

LITTLE TIGER

LONDON

CATERPILLAR BOOKS
An imprint of the Little Tiger Group
www.littletiger.co.uk
1 Coda Studios, 189 Munster Road, London SW6 6AW
Imported into the EEA by Penguin Random House Ireland,
Morrison Chambers, 32 Nassau Street, Dublin D02 YH68
Originally published in 2021
First published in Great Britain 2022
Text by Jonny Marx • Text copyright © Caterpillar Books Ltd 2021
Illustration copyright © Christiane Engel 2021
A CIP catalogue record for this book
is available from the British Library
All rights reserved • Printed in China
ISBN: 978-1-83891-342-7
CPB/2200/1994/1121
1 3 5 7 9 10 8 6 4 2

TOUCANS

A toucan's iconic beak is mostly hollow.
Inside, it looks a bit like **HONEYCOMB**, with
lots of interlocking shapes giving the beak strength.

A toucan's **TONGUE** looks like a **FEATHER**.
It helps flick food down the bird's throat.

Excluding its feathers, a toucan's **BEAK** is
roughly the same size as the rest of its body.

A toucan has a big appetite. Every day,
it gobbles **DOZENS OF FRUITS** whole.

BUTTERFLIES

A butterfly starts life as a **CATERPILLAR**. When the caterpillar is strong enough, it creates a tough pod in which to live, called a **CHRYSALIS**. After several days or weeks, the creature reappears from the chrysalis — but this time it can **FLY**!

The **LARGEST** butterfly in the world is as big as a dinner plate.

A butterfly can't flap its wings if it gets too cold.

Butterflies sometimes sip water from muddy puddles to get **MINERALS** and **SALTS**.

FROGS

Frogs start life as a **JELLY-LIKE** slime called **FROGSPAWN**. Eventually, the frogspawn hatches and **TADPOLES** swim out!

The tadpoles slowly start to transform into **FROGS**. First, they grow small legs, then arms. The tail shrinks and the frogs begin to climb and hop, rather than swim.

Frogs belong to a group of creatures called **AMPHIBIANS**. Amphibians require a wet or moisture-rich environment in order to survive.

They soak up water through their skin, so they don't need to drink.

Some frogs are **POISONOUS**. Even touching certain species could make a person very sick.

BATS

The bat is the only mammal that can **FLY**.

Bats digest their food quickly. Some can eat and poop a meal in just **20 MINUTES**.

Bats emit sounds to **SENSE** the world around them. This is called **ECHOLOCATION**. They can catch prey in complete darkness by locating its presence using **SOUND**. The best hunters can catch more than **1,000 INSECTS** in an hour.

Like bears, some bats **HIBERNATE** (rest for a long period of time). Some can also survive extreme cold, using their wings like a blanket.

CROCODILES

Crocodiles are arguably the animal kingdom's most successful **PREDATOR**. They have existed almost unchanged since the age of **DINOSAURS**.

The **SALTWATER CROCODILE** has the strongest bite of any living animal. The muscles the crocodile uses to open its mouth, however, are incredibly **WEAK** and can be trapped shut with just an elastic band.

Crocodiles can't sweat, so in order to keep cool, a crocodile will open its mouth and **PANT** like a dog.

The saltwater crocodile is the planet's **LARGEST REPTILE**. It can grow to a length of more than 6m (20ft) — that's as long as a **MINIBUS**!

SNAKES

Snakes are **REPTILES**. They are cold-blooded, which means they have to use their environment to keep warm.

Some species of snake can eat creatures much larger than you might expect. The rock python can stretch its jaws wide enough to eat a **PIG**! It can't chew, so it has to eat its prey whole.

The majority of snake species hatch from **EGGS**.

Some snakes live in **SWAMPS** or in the **SEA**.

PLANTS AND FLOWERS

The *Rafflesia arnoldii* plant **SMELLS** like rotting meat. This pungent scent attracts the insects and creatures that the plant feasts on.

Giant bamboo shoots can grow up to 30cm (12in) a day, soaring to a height of **30M (100FT)** when fully grown. These plants flower just once every **40 YEARS**.

Venus fly traps are **CARNIVOROUS**! They eat insects.

Pitcher plants produce a liquid that can **DIGEST** all sorts of animals, including frogs.

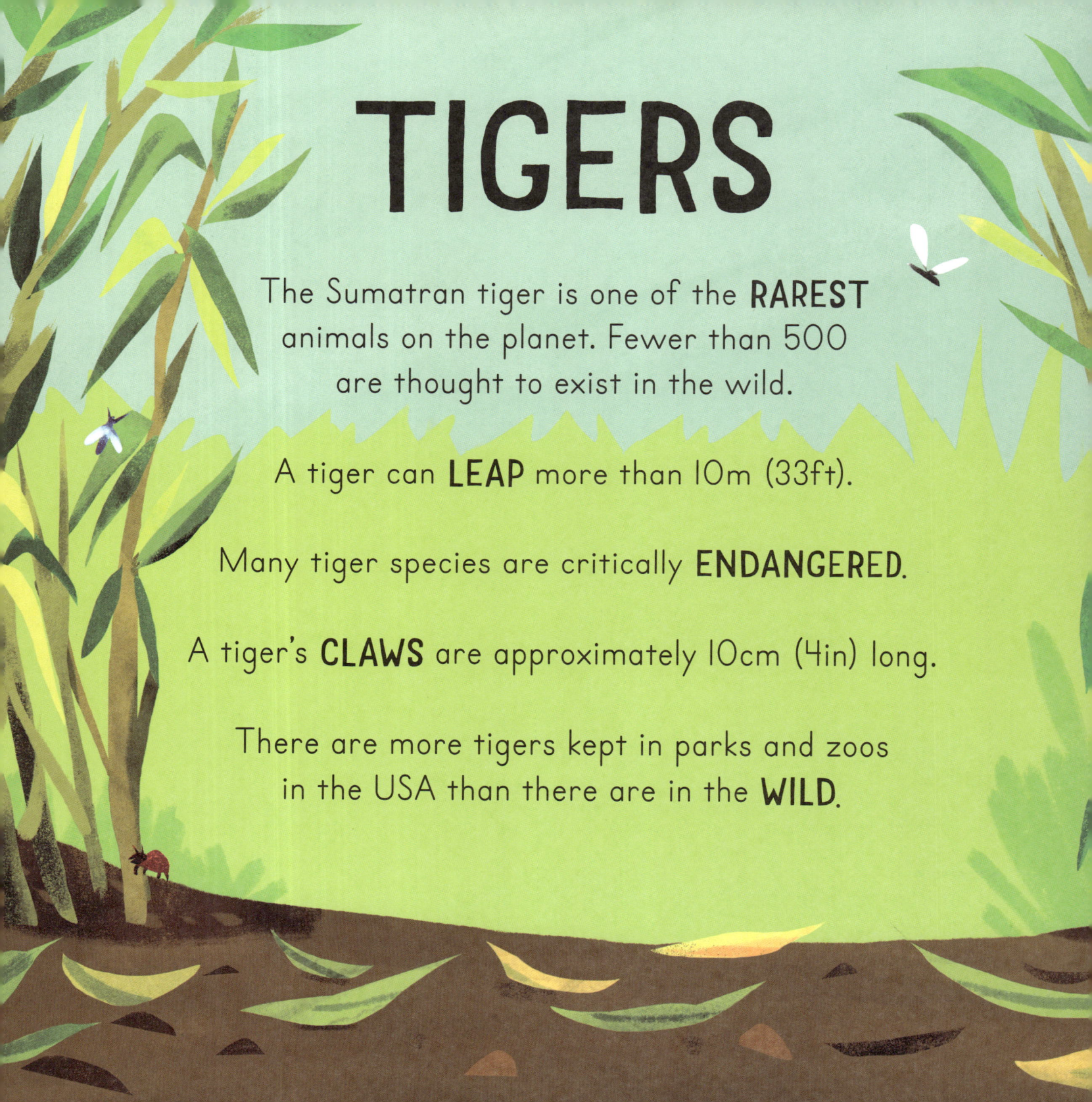

TIGERS

The Sumatran tiger is one of the **RAREST** animals on the planet. Fewer than 500 are thought to exist in the wild.

A tiger can **LEAP** more than 10m (33ft).

Many tiger species are critically **ENDANGERED**.

A tiger's **CLAWS** are approximately 10cm (4in) long.

There are more tigers kept in parks and zoos in the USA than there are in the **WILD**.

PARROTS

The **BUFF-FACED PYGMY PARROT** is about the length of a human finger. The **HYACINTH MACAW**, on the other hand, can grow to a length of more than 1m (3ft).

Some parrot species can mimic human **SPEECH**. The world record-holding bird could recite more than 1,700 different words.

The **KAKAPO** is a flightless species of parrot. It lives in New Zealand and can weigh as much as a cat.

Parrots can live for half a century.

SPOTTER'S CHECKLIST

Tick off all of the items you find next time you go on an outdoor adventure.

LILY PAD ⚪

EGG ⚪

BEETLE ⚪

FROG ⚪

NEST ⚪

FLOWER ⚪

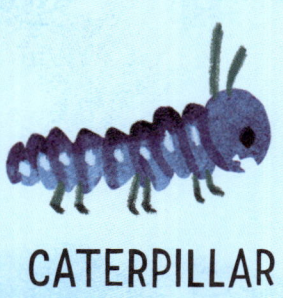

CATERPILLAR ⚪

BUTTERFLY ⚪

BAT ⚪

BEETLES

1
2
4
7
6
3
5
10
8
9

TOUCANS

1
3
4
9
10
5
11
2
6
8
13
14
7
12
16
15

BUTTERFLIES

FROGS

BATS

CROCODILES

SNAKES

PLANTS AND FLOWERS